T0005031

How Do I
Plan
Well?

**Helen Cox Cannons
and Angela Royston**

CHERITON
CHILDREN'S BOOKS

Please visit our website, www.cheritonchildrensbooks.com to see more of our high-quality books.

First Edition

Published in 2022 by **Cheriton Children's Books**
PO Box 7258, Bridgnorth WV16 9ET, UK

© 2022 Cheriton Children's Books

Authors: Helen Cox Cannons and Angela Royston
Designer: Paul Myerscough
Editor: Jennifer Sanderson
Picture Researcher: Rachel Blount
Proofreader: Wendy Scavuzzo

Picture credits: Cover: Shutterstock/Asier Romero. Inside: p1: Shutterstock/LightField Studios; p4: Shutterstock/Viktoriia Hnatiuk; p5: Shutterstock/Kiselev Andrey Valerevich; p6: Shutterstock/Dragon Images; p7: Shutterstock/BAZA Production; p8: Shutterstock/Studio Romantic; p9: Shutterstock/Prostock-studio; p10: Shutterstock/Cat Simpson; p11: Shutterstock/Daisy Daisy; p12: Shutterstock/sirtravelalot; p13: Shutterstock/Alena Ozerova; p14: Shutterstock/insta_photos; p15: Shutterstock/Veja; p16: Shutterstock/Yakobchuk Viacheslav; p17: Shutterstock/LightField Studios; p18: Shutterstock/Gorodenkoff; p19: Shutterstock/Ruslan Huzau; p20: Shutterstock/Roman Samborskyi; p21: Shutterstock/LightField Studios; p22: Shutterstock/Lapina; p23: Shutterstock/Asife; p24: Shutterstock/sirtravelalot; p25: Shutterstock/Ronnachai Palas; p26: Shutterstock/Denis Moskvinov; p27: Shutterstock/Pixel-Shot; p28: Shutterstock/Diego Cervo; p29: Shutterstock/Mauricio Graiki.

Printed in the United States of America

Contents

Help! Why Should I Plan?

#Help! You've got your math class this morning and you haven't done your homework. You were going to get to it on the weekend—after you went to the mall, hung out with your friends, and went to a party...Now it's Monday morning, and you are freaking out. If this sounds like a page from your life, it's time to stop panicking and start planning!

Planning—It's a Priority!

Planning is all about prioritizing. That means deciding what is most important. For example, you know you need to do your homework, but you also want to watch your favorite TV show. Both might be important to you, but if you miss your homework **deadline**, you'll get into trouble at school. That means you need to make your homework the first thing you do. It is your priority. Once it is done, you can sit back, relax, and watch as much TV as you like! It's just a case of planning your priorities.

You Can Hack It!

Can you think of some situations in which being able to plan well would make your life easier? What are they?

Partying can be a priority at holiday times, such as Christmas. But at other times, homework should come first!

#Help!

What's So Great About Planning?

Planning is one of the most important skills that you can learn. Good planning makes sure that your life runs smoothly, and helps you achieve many important things. Here are some things planning can help you do:

- Organize your time. By planning well, you can allow yourself enough time to do the things you need to do.
- Do things to the best of your **ability**. By planning, you can make sure that you think through what you are doing and how you are going to do it. That means you complete tasks well.
- Improve your relationships with other people. No one likes being let down! If you are always late when meeting others, or forget to show up, they will be annoyed. Planning helps you be on time, and keep your friends!

Chapter One
Help! How Do I Make a Plan?

#Don'tPanic! When you've got a lot of things to do, it's easy to freak out. But writing it all down in a plan helps you feel in control. It also helps you decide which order to do tasks in. Being organized means you stay on top of what you have to do and when you have to do it by. Feels better already, right?!

Break It Down

Most plans begin with a checklist. This is a list of what you have to do. Writing a checklist often needs to be broken down into different steps. For example, people often follow a recipe when they are cooking. The recipe tells them what they need, what to do, and what order to do it in. When you are making a checklist, try treating it like a recipe. For example, a checklist for planning an art project might go like this:

- Collect materials: pencils, eraser, paints, brushes
- Choose what to paint: my dog
- Order of task: first, sketch my dog, then color my sketch with paints, finally, leave to dry

A checklist will help you **focus** on how best to complete your task.

How Do I Use a Checklist?

Here's how to get the best out of your checklist of tasks:

- *Check it off*: Check off each thing on your list when you've done it.
- *Keep going*: As you keep checking things off, you'll start to see progress as your list gets shorter.
- *Keep track*: Check how much you still have to do and figure out how much time you need to complete it.

#Hack: Planning tasks leaves you time to do the things you really want to do.

Chores—Check! Fun—Double-Check!

Checklists are great for planning your time. A checklist can help you figure out how long tasks will take, and how much time you have left for other things, such as having fun. Write down all your tasks for the day, how long they will take, and in what order to do them. That way, you know what to do first, when you will finish, and when you can start having fun!

What Do I Do If My Plan Goes Wrong?

Sometimes, even the best plans go wrong. Perhaps you've planned a surprise birthday picnic for your best friend at the park. But it's started raining! You may have planned perfectly for an event, but some things are out of your control. What do you do when things go wrong? Here are some tips on how to be prepared so, if things do go wrong, you can still get it right.

What Could Go Wrong, Right?!

When you plan an event, try to think ahead about what might go wrong. For example, you've planned a trip to the park, but it's closed. What do you do? You use your backup plan—your Plan B. That might involve inviting your friends to your home instead of going to the park, or going to see a movie instead. A Plan B helps you plan ahead in case things don't work out perfectly.

Plan B can be just as great as Plan A. Maybe even better!

You Can Hack It!

Have you ever planned something that has gone wrong? How would having a Plan B have helped in that situation?

Plans for tasks can go wrong, too. For example, you have a list of chores to do but you're running out of time to complete them. What do you do? Simply figure out which chores are the most important. Then you can do the other chores on a different day when you have more time available. Simple, huh?

#Help!

How Can I Avoid Disaster?

Sometimes, you have to change your plans, whether you like it or not. Other times, you can plan to avoid disasters. Here's how best to keep your plans on track:

- *Don't be late*: If you start on time, you'll give yourself the best chance of achieving something.
- *Keep to the plan*: Don't get **sidetracked** into doing something else. It might help to switch your cell phone off!
- *Be ready to change*: Make sure your plan is working and, if not, be prepared to adjust it.
- *Take a break and get help*: If something is more difficult than you expected, get help with it or leave it until later.

How Do I Plan to Be Ready?

Are you always late for school? Always leaving homework at home? Hitting the snooze button and missing the bus? Then it's time to take control! If you can organize yourself now, you'll cinch it when you are older. Here are some top tips for getting to school on time—every time.

You've Got to Figure It Out!

Figure out how long it actually takes you to get up and get ready for school. For example, how long does it take to get dressed in the morning? How long do you need to eat breakfast and to pack your schoolbag? How long do you normally take to brush your teeth? Set an alarm clock to wake you up in good time. That way, you'll make sure you start the day early enough to get everything done on time.

I'm So Sorted!

Save time by getting as much as possible ready the night before. For example, get your clothes out for the next day. Check what activities you have for the next day, so you can pack your bag with everything you will need. That way, you will have less to do in the morning. You may even be able to grab a few more minutes in bed!

#Hack: Make sure you go to bed on time. It will make getting up for school so much easier!

Don't forget the extra things you need on particular days. If you have a dance class, pack the clothes that you will need.

#Help!

How Do I Plan Ahead?

Make a checklist of the things that you need to take to school. Before you go to bed, check that everything is ready for the next day:

- Have you done all your homework?
- Have you packed your schoolbag?
- Have you got the clothes you need for sports or other activities?
- Do you need to take a musical instrument?
- Do you need money?
- Did you pack your lunch?

OK, you've learned to plan what you have to do. Good job! Now let's figure out how to plan what you *want* to do. That's right—F.U.N.—you need to plan it in! Making time to relax is important. It not only allows your body the rest that it needs, but it gives you time to do the things you enjoy the most. You just need to find a good balance between work, rest, and play.

Relax—It's All Part of the Plan!

While you are at school, your day is mostly planned for you. You don't have to think about what to do next. When school is over, though, you may have after-school activities. For example, you might have a sport club or music practice—and they need to be planned, too.

Try to plan your after-school time carefully. You need to finish any activities early enough to find time to relax—and get to bed on time. Losing important sleep time will just make you tired the next day. And that is definitely not part of the plan!

Band practice is great—but so is finishing on time.

Good planning allows you to enjoy your downtime. Well, you've earned it!

#Help!

How Do I Make the Most of My Time?

Whether you are planning what to do for a day, a whole weekend, or an evening, use these tips to help you make the most of your time:

- Do you have to do something at a fixed time? If so, allow extra time to meet the deadline.
- Decide what you can fit in before and after the fixed-time events.
- Don't try to fit in too much. You could end up rushing around and not enjoying anything.
- Include some time to chill!

Chapter Two
Help! How Do I Plan for School?

#Homework—Let'sDoThis! OK, homework might not always be fun. And it may not be easy. But, unless you get kidnapped by aliens, it's not going away anytime soon. In fact, as you get older, the chances are you will get more homework...Yup, that's right! Feel like searching for UFOs? We've got a better plan...

Hey, Homework, Same Time Tomorrow?

If possible, always try to do your homework in the same place and at the same time every night. Then it will become a **routine**. Choose a quiet place where you will not be **interrupted** or **distracted**. You will be able to complete your homework more quickly and on time if you focus on it quietly.

#Hack: Homework needs complete focus—don't allow yourself to get distracted.

How Do I Manage My Homework Time?

To find out how long you should be taking to do homework, multiply your grade by 10. For example, you should be spending 40 minutes in grade 4, and 50 minutes in grade 5. If you are taking longer than this, ask your teacher how long you should take. You might be doing more than you need to. Here are some tips for working faster:

- *Think it through*: First, figure out what you are going to do.
- *Focus your mind*: **Concentrate** on what you are doing.
- *Take a break*: If you get tired, take a short break and have a healthy snack before you continue.

Don't Put It Off!

If you have more than one thing to do for homework, decide in which order you will do them. Most people think that you should do the most difficult piece of work first, before your brain becomes tired. That way, you can really focus on the task. Later, you can do less-difficult tasks, that are still manageable even if you are tired.

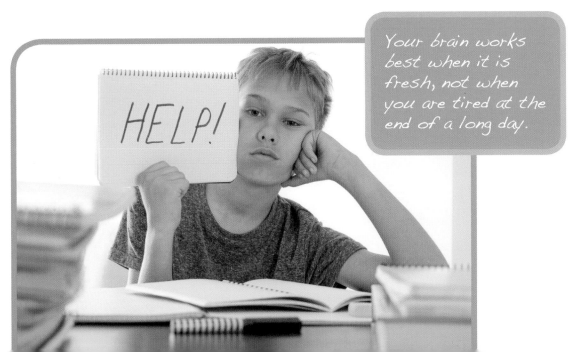

Your brain works best when it is fresh, not when you are tired at the end of a long day.

How Do I Plan a Project?

Next up: planning a big project. How does that sound? Great? Or not so great? Well, however you feel about it, the first thing to do is figure out where to start. Try splitting up a big project up into stages. These usually include a **timetable**, **research**, writing, and **presentation**. Let's take a look.

Timing Is Everything

Make a timetable to show what you have to do by when and plan each stage separately. This will help you finish everything on time.

Research It

When planning your research, make a list of what you need to find out, and then decide where to find the information you need. That is most likely to be either on the Internet or from books in a library.

Great results come from great planning! What are you waiting for?!

#Hack: If you are feeling **overwhelmed** by a research project, ask your friends to help.

Write It Up, Hand It In

If you have a lot to write, split it up into different sections so you don't feel overwhelmed. Then you can put them in order. Always start with your **introduction**. Also think about whether typing it on a computer or writing it by hand is best for your project.

#Help!

How Do I Do Research on the Internet?

The Internet is great, but we need to use it carefully. Why? Well, many websites are unreliable. Be aware of false news and double-check that the information you have is factually correct. Also, always write the information down in your own words. Follow these tips:

- Use websites that belong to organizations you can trust to be accurate. Choose websites that end with .org, for example, rather than .com.
- Be aware of **forums** and websites that offer opinions rather than facts.
- Do not copy and paste text you have found on the Internet. This is called **plagiarism**.

17

How Do I Plan for Tests?

Have you already had to prepare for and take some tests at school? Does your teacher ever give quizzes in class? As you get older, you will take more tests and exams. The good news? Great planning will help you do your best.

Ready for Anything

The best way to prepare for a written test is to **review** what you are expected to know. Learn the facts you have been taught. If it is a spelling test, practice your spelling words beforehand until you know them inside out. If you have a music test, be sure to rehearse well ahead of time so you are confident on the day. Index cards can be a helpful tool for learning facts in subjects such as science. Write the name of the topic on the front, then note key facts about the topic on the back.

If you plan for a test, you will feel more confident when you take it.

How Do I Take a Test?

#Help!

You've done the preparation, and now it's time for the test. What can you do to give yourself the best chance of doing well? Most important of all is to stay calm. Here are some other tips to follow:

- *Don't forget to breathe!*: Before you begin, take some deep breaths and focus on what you are about to do.
- *Read the question*: Begin by reading the question carefully before you start to answer it.
- *Make sure you understand*: Be sure you are clear about what is being asked of you.

Hiding Doesn't Help!

If you know you have a test coming up, ignoring it will just make things worse. It's best to face it, and plan how you are going to prepare for the test. Once you put together a plan and start to work on it, everything will feel far less scary. It works! Really!

#Hack: Hiding under the duvet and hoping a test will go away won't help. Planning will!

19

Chapter Three

Help! How Do I Plan My Life?

#Let'sTalkMoney! Perhaps you get a weekly **allowance** or you are given money for doing chores. Perhaps you would like to make more money! Learning how to spend and save will help make your money go further. And learning how to plan your **finances** is a skill that will set you up for life.

You Don't Have to Spend It All!

Do you spend most of your money on snacks and sodas, or are you saving up for a cell phone, tablet, or something else you really want? If you're used to spending all your money, try saving a little each week. After a while, you will have saved a larger amount to spend on other things.

If you are already saving, check that your plan will work. For example, if you are saving $1 a week, how long will it take to save the amount you need?

You Can Hack It!

What little things could you stop spending your money on? How much could you then save?

If you save money regularly, you can use it for things that you really like, such as going to the movies.

How Can I Manage My Money?

Set yourself a **budget**. It will help you decide how to use the money that you regularly receive. Here are some basic steps to help you budget:

- Write down how much money you receive every week.
- Make a list of the things you have to buy and how much they cost. For example, you may have birthday presents to buy for your friends.
- Figure out how much that leaves you to spend every week.
- Divide this amount among extra things you want to buy or save for. More expensive items will take longer to save for.

How Do I Plan a Party?

It's party time! But where do you start when it comes to planning your party? The first thing to do is come up with a theme. Whether it's a Halloween, fancy dress, or outdoor activity party, you'll want you and all your friends to have the best time—so let's get started!

If you are planning a theme party, make sure you allow time to make decorations and costumes.

What's There to Plan?

The main things to plan for a party are the place, date, the invitations, food, and activities. You need to plan this as early as possible to make sure you have everything in place before you send out the invitations. After all, you don't want to tell everyone the party is in a certain place and then find out it's already booked that day! Discuss everything with your parents as you go along.

How Do I Make Invitations?

#Help!

You can buy packs of invitations on which you only have to fill in the details, but it is fun to make your own. If you do this, these are the things you need to put on the invitations:

- Name of the person you're inviting.
- The date and time, and the theme, if there is one.
- The address or place where the party will be.
- Your name, so everyone knows it's your party!

What Kind of Party?

Next, think about what you want to do at your party. You could include a treasure hunt, or going to the movies. A Halloween party could include costumes, bobbing for apples, and maybe going trick-or-treating. What kind of food will you have? Perhaps the whole party is a visit to a favorite restaurant or a swimming pool that you like.

You Can Hack It!

How would you plan a surprise party? What important things would you need to build into your plan to make it a success?

How Do I Plan to Help?

Do you have a favorite **charity** that you like to support? Perhaps you want to help protect **endangered animals**, or help protect the **environment**. You can help your favorite charity by raising money for it. This is called fundraising. Sounds good? But how do you go about it? Well, like everything, with a little planning, it is easy!

Money Made Easy

One of the easiest ways to raise money is to hold a sale at school, or a garage or yard sale at home. (Make sure you get **permission** first!) You could ask people to make cakes and cookies for a bake sale, or ask them to bring items such as toys, books, or DVDs to sell. You could ask your friends and family to help you sell the items, too.

Having a bake sale is a great way to earn extra money—as long as you don't eat all the cakes...

Cleaning cars can be a great—and really fun—way to earn money.

Sponsor Me!

You could organize a challenge, such as running as many times as possible around the park, or a **sponsored** car wash event in which you wash as many cars as you can. You then ask people to sponsor you a certain amount for every **circuit** of the park you run, or every car you wash. Sponsored events are a great way to raise money and be active at the same time!

#Help!

How Do I Collect the Money?

Collecting the money is the most important part of the event!

- If you are holding a sale, have a bag or cash box for keeping the money safe.
- After a sponsored event, you need to collect the money from your sponsors. Figure out what people owe you or your friends based on what you or they have achieved.
- Tell everyone involved the grand total!

How Do I Plan a Vacation?

School's out! The summer vacation is here, but how are you going to spend it? There are usually activities, summer school classes, or sports you can do in your neighborhood. Perhaps you and your family have a vacation planned. Or maybe you could go to a summer camp that could take you away for a week or more. It's time to plan!

It's All in the Detail

If you decide to go to summer camp, you and your parents need to **reserve** your place. Then, you need to figure out how to get there. Will you go by car, bus, or train? Plan your route and write down the travel times if you're going on public transportation. Closer to the time you leave, you can plan other details, such as what to take with you.

Amazing vacations don't happen by chance—they take a lot of planning. Just ask your parents or guardians!

What Shall I Pack?

How do you make sure that you pack everything you need but don't take too much? The answer is to make a list. Your list might include items like these:

- Change of clothes
- Swimsuit
- Towel
- Nightwear
- Toiletry bag with toothbrush, toothpaste, soap, washcloth, etc.
- Hairbrush or comb
- Sunscreen

Learn from Parents (Yes, Really!)

If your whole family is taking a vacation together, your parents will make all the arrangements. You can learn a lot by taking an interest in the plans they make. What do they have to do before you all leave? How does this help you with your own planning?

#Hack: Figure out exactly what you need (and don't need!) to take on vacation before you pack.

Help! How Do I Plan My Future?

#PlanForLife! As you get older, you will have more things to deal with, and planning will help you take control of them. The more you plan, the more it will become part of your everyday life. Let's get a head start now by learning what type of things you might need to plan for in the future.

Making Bigger Plans

As you get older, you will probably have to make bigger plans. For example, you may choose to go to college. You will then need to plan what college to go to, and what to study there. Once you leave college, you will begin work. Then you will need to plan what type of job you want to do, and how to apply for it. You may choose to run your own business. And your plans may even change halfway through—remember, that's where your Plan B comes in!

Going to college is a big step in a young person's life. With careful planning, it can be an amazing experience.

And finally—
if you start
planning now,
you'll be an
expert planner
for life!

Planning Forever

While making grown-up decisions may sound **daunting**,
it helps to know that anything can be achieved if you
have a plan. You have years and years before you need
to make big decisions. Just keep on planning and, by
the time you need to make big plans, you'll be a pro!

#Help!

How Can I Be a Great Planner?

Here are some top tips to help you stay on track:

- *Keep a checklist*: Don't forget to make a checklist—it
  will help you keep track of your plans.
- *Have a Plan B*: Remember, sometimes things go wrong
  and you might have to change your plans.
- *Plan your time*: Allow enough time to carry out your
  plans, and don't forget to plan ahead.
- *Do your research*: Make sure you know what you are
  planning and why you are planning.
- *Plan to have fun!*: Don't forget to plan your downtime.
  After all, with all that planning, you've earned it!

Glossary

ability how able a person is to do something

allowance an amount of money someone is allowed and given on a regular basis

budget a plan for estimating how money received will be used, spent, and saved

charity an organization that collects money, which it spends to help people, animals, and other good causes

circuit a circular movement that ends where it began

concentrate give your full attention or effort to something

daunting frightening and overwhelming

deadline a date or time by which something must be done by

distracted had one's concentration drawn away from something

endangered animals animals that are in danger of becoming extinct—that is, of dying out altogether

environment the natural world

finances money resources

focus concentrate on something

forums Internet message boards

interrupted stopped partway through doing or saying something

introduction the very first part of a piece of writing

overwhelmed feeling unable to cope

permission being allowed to do something

plagiarism copying and using someone else's words and passing them off as your own

presentation communication and explanation of information or ideas

research find out about something

reserve to set aside

review go over information already learned

routine a fixed way of doing things

sidetracked diverted or moved away from the correct course

sponsored given money in support of a cause

timetable an ordered sequence of events and times at which they take place

Find Out More

Books

Hillard, Stephanie. *Plan a Yard-Work Business* (Be Your Own Boss). PowerKids Press, 2020.

Newman, Catherine. *How to Be a Person: 65 Hugely Useful, Super-Important Skills to Learn before You're Grown Up.* Storey Publishing, 2020.

Sherman Pearl, Melissa, and David A. Sherman. *Kids Saving the Rainforest: Charities Started by Kids!* Cherry Lake Publishing, 2017.

Websites

This website about planning homework is written for teenagers, but you can find some useful tips here to help you now as well as later. **kidshealth.org/teen/school_jobs/school/homework.html**

This website for kids gives you good advice on how to manage your allowance. It includes comments posted by kids. **www.cyh.com/HealthTopics/HealthTopicDetailsKids. aspx?p=335&np=282&id=2235**

This website about how to plan a party is written for parents, but it has lots of advice and information that you can use, too. **www.kidspartyfun.com/pages/planningguide.html**

Publisher's note to educators and parents:
All the websites featured above have been carefully reviewed to ensure that they are suitable for students. However, many websites change often, and we cannot guarantee that a site's future contents will continue to meet our high standards of educational value. Please be advised that students should be closely monitored whenever they access the Internet.

Index

About the Authors

Helen Cox Cannons has written many informative and entertaining books for children. Angela Royston is a hugely experienced author who has written hundreds of wonderful books for children. Both are expert planners!